Introduction

This book introduces another unique tool, the 'Varipin' pin, and the Flower Swan, both designed by Rosa V I also introduce my version of Rosa's Swan cake. Tl One Orchid by Sandra Townsend. I also show various including Kathy Moore's spectacular Peacock Cake. cutters to make a Camellia.

The Tools.

General Notes: Non-stick. One of their most useful aspects is their non-stick property, which is inherent in the design and material used. It is not a surface finish and, therefore, cannot wear off. It also means they cut cleanly, without fuzzy edges. They should **NOT** be 'scrubbed' on the board or twisted.

Materials. All the tools can be used with any soft material such as flowerpaste, sugarpaste, Permapaste, marzipan, modelling chocolate, plasticine, modelling clay, etc.

Temperature. Normally hand washing in warm soapy water is all that is required. They will withstand boiling water or the dishwasher without deforming.

Handles. All the cutters have handles or fit comfortably into your hand, which allows you to exert firm pressure over the whole of the cutting edges.

Stability. They will not rust, corrode, deform or wear out with normal useage.

Marking. All the tools are permanently marked to aid easy identification.

Metal. The cutters are delicate and should not be brought into contact with sharp metal objects which may damage the cutting edges or surfaces. i.e. keep them separated from metal cutters.

Hygiene. The materials meet the appropriate EEC regulations for food hygiene.

Endorsement. All the items are personally endorsed and used by PAT ASHBY, our Technical Director, who is one of the leading teachers of sugarcraft in the UK and is an International judge, author and demonstrator.

* These cutters, as with all Orchard cutters, can be used very effectively with an airdrying non-edible paste (Cold Porcelain) such as Orchard 'Permapaste'.

The New Tools.
(see Illustration 1)

1. The 'Varipin'. This textured rolling pin is 10¾" x ⅞" dia. in clear non-stick plastic and gives a delightful fabric like effect to any soft material when rolled firmly over the surface. It can be used to texture your cake board covering, the frills or lace round a cake, or for novelty effects such as water or bark.

2. The Flower Swan Cutters (SW1,SW2,SW3 and Moulds SW4, SW5)) These attactive cutters and moulds enable you to create a dramatic swan decoration, as you can see on Pages 4 -6.

3. The Large Five-petal Cutters (F6B, F6C) 3½" and 4" dia. allow you to create some of the larger flowers easily, such as roses, peonies and camellias, as illustrated on Pages 30-31.

4. The Mini Turntable is a very convenient 4¼" dia.lightweight turntable which slips easily into your box or bag for class and can support a 60lb weight.

1

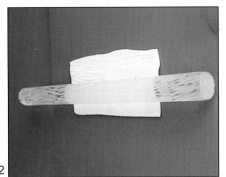

2

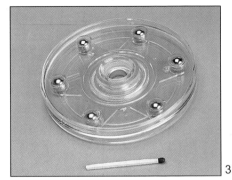

3

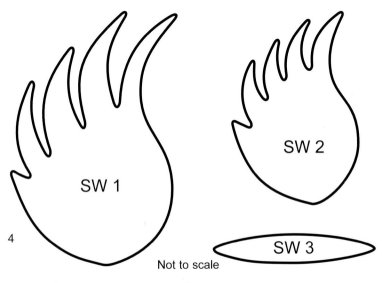

SW 1

SW 2

SW 3

4

Not to scale

5

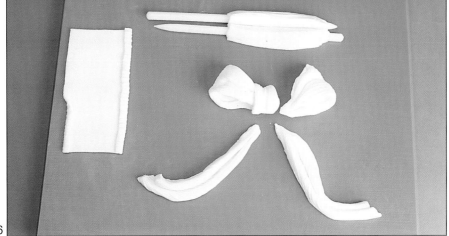

6

How to make the Bow Cake.
(see Illustration 5)

The Bow. This is made in sections and can be any size you require. The dimensions given are for the 6" square cake in the picture. The paste is flowerpaste A or similar.

1. Roll out the paste with a smooth rolling pin a little thicker than normal.

   Then roll over it with the veined 'Varipin' (Rosa's Roller), pressing firmly to get all the embossing onto the paste. Cut a rectangle - half the bow - approx. 2" wide x 7" long. Turn the paste over and fold a little 'hem' down each side. Stick down with rose water. Turn the paste right side up. Pop onto a kitchen roll tissue to reduce the mess!

2. Dust the paste with a lustre dust of choice -say Orchard Majestic Gold.

3. To make a fold (or ruffle) in the bow, place 2 small rolling pins(Slimpin or similar) longitudinally in the centre under the paste. Gently smooth the paste into the ruffles with the balling tool, squeeze the ends and remove the pins. Squeeze the ends of the paste again inwards and stick in place with 'glue'. Turn over and fold one end over towards the other to form the half bow. Trim off at an angle. Support with 'cloud drift' or a film container. Leave to dry.(see Illustration 6).

4. Repeat Steps 1 to 3 for the other half of the bow.

5. For the two ties, repeat Steps 1 and 2, but approx. 1½" x 8" long each. Trim the ends to suit. Drape them over the cake and prop with 'cloud drift' to give a flowing look.

6. Stick the two half bows onto the cake with paste glue where the ties meet.

7. Prepare a small piece of paste as in Steps 1 and 2 and wrap over the join of the half bows to make the knot.

8. To make the Cerise Chrysanthemums see Orchard Book 6 Page 29.

   The Oak leaves are in Book 5 Page 38.

9. Decorate the bottom of the cake with a strip of lace cut out from the veined paste with the Orchard Lace Cutter, straight blade in Hole 2. See Book 8.

How to make the Flower Swan.
(see Illustrations 7 & 8). *Cake illustration by Sandra Townsend.*

1. Head and neck. This can be made by hand or with a mould. Roll out a thin sausage of White flowerpaste(see recipe Page 40) or pastillage about 3" long and press the end to form a beak. Leave the next section to represent the head and thin down the rest of the sausage to represent the neck. Glue and insert a White 26 gauge wire into the base (see Illustration 9). Make a tiny indentation on either side of the face with a cocktail stick to represent eyes. Leave to dry on a sponge. When dry paint the face - Yellow beak and pipe the eyes Black. Leave to dry.

1a. Alternatively make the head and neck with the Orchard Mould SW5 using White flowerpaste or pastillage. Press a sausage of paste into each half of the mould, level off with a thin spatula, pressing as you go, and wiping the spatula if there is any surplus paste on it.Apply rose water glue to one half of the neck. Press the two halves together. Peel from the mould, glue and insert a White 24 gauge wire into the base. Leave to dry on a sponge (not on a hard surface). Should there be any gaps or marks fill in with Royal Icing and smooth with a damp finger.

2. Tail Feathers. Roll out White flowerpaste with a thicker edge (to allow a wire to be inserted). Cut out 9 feathers per swan with the Orchard Swan Cutter SW3. Make some spares. Place on the Orchard pad PD1 and soften the edges of the feathers with the

7

balling tool OP1. Firmly drag the small end of the tool from the tip to the base to curl. Mark a line down the centre with the pointed end of the petal veining tool OP2. Glue florists rose wire with paste glue, insert into each base and squeeze firmly. Gently squeeze the sides of the feather inwards to cup slightly. Bend gently lengthways and leave to dry in a curved position. When dry wrap a small piece of rose wire tightly round the wire of 3 feathers and repeat twice for the other 6. Dust with Orchard Bridal Satin.

Tape all 3 sets with ½ width florists tape and then tape all 3 together with 2 slightly lower down. Bend wire back to assist with assembly.

3. Side wings. Roll out White flowerpaste with a thicker edge. Cut out 2 side wings each with Orchard Swan Cutters SW1 & SW2. Glue and insert a 26 gauge wire into the base. Soften the edges with the balling tool on the Orchard pad. Press the wings onto the Orchard Feather veiner SW4 (remembering the opposite sides). Ball in the centre to curve. Leave to set in a slightly curved position, say, in an apple tray. Dust with Orchard Bridal Satin.

4. Assembly. Tape the neck and side feathers (SW1,SW2) together with full width tape as Illustration 9. Then slot in and tape on the tail feathers (SW3). Gently steam the whole assembly.

5. Use a blue 70mm Orchard flower pick to safely attach your swan to a cake.

8

9

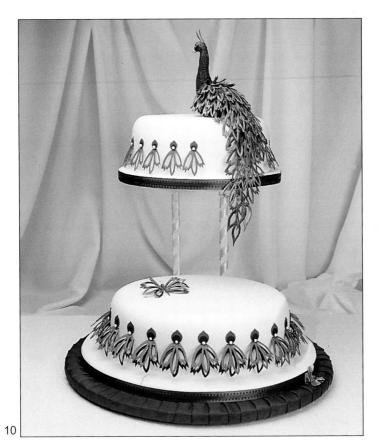

10

11

How to make the Peacock Cake.
(see Illustration 10)

This stunning cake was designed by Kathy Moore using ,basically, the Lace Leaf Cutters. You will need an 8" and 11" round fruit cake, and 10", 14" and 17" cake drums.

Note: If you wish to use the ribbons or fabric, match the colour of the pastes to the ribbons rather than the other way round!

1. Method. Cover the cakes with marzipan and sugarpaste and place them centrally on the boards. Measure the distance between the covered cake and the edge of the board and roll out a long strip of sugarpaste slightly wider and long enough to go right round the board. Smooth paste with a smoother, and cut a straight line along one edge. Lightly moisten the cake board with cooled boiled water and place the strip of paste on the board with the cut edge next to the cake. Continue all the way round the board until the strip ends meet. Overlap and cut to make a neat join. Smooth gently with your hands to erase the join line. Trim the edges of the cake board with a sharp knife and stroke the outer edge with the palm of your hand to give a nice rounded finish. Pipe a snail's trail round the base of each cake with a No.0 tube. Leave to dry. Using a Pritt Stick or something similar, run the stick glue round the cake board edge and attach the Jade ribbon. Glue the back of the narrow Blue ribbon and and stick on top of the Jade ribbon, making sure it is central and level all the way round.

2. Peacock. Form a large cone from 6ozs (170g) of pastillage. Elongate the pointed end by rolling between the palms of your hands, to form the neck and then bend the top of the neck over to form the head. Pinch the end of the head to form the beak. Bend neck and head to give a bird shape. Shape tail end to a slight point. (Don't worry about the body shape as it will be covered with 'feathers'). Place a dowel halfway through the body and then push the dowel into a block of oasis and leave to dry. (see Illustration 11) Paint the peacock with thin Royal Icing coloured with Blues and Greens. Before it dries, scratch the neck with a pin to give a feathered effect. Leave to dry. Dust with Orchard Super Blue and Super Jade lustre colours and paint in the eyes with Black paste colour or use a Black food colour pen. Measure the depth of the cake and, leaving the dowel in the peacock, cut the dowel to this length. Insert into the cake and secure with a little Royal Icing underneath the body. Leave to dry.

3. Feathers.(see Illustration 12) Make up about 2 - 3ozs(80g) flowerpaste to match each colour of ribbon. Roll out the pastes and cut out plenty of Orchard Lace Leaves LL1,LL2,LL3 & LL4 in both colours...Keep some of the small centre pieces and shape these over a small rolling pin. Starting at the back of the peacock's body, attach the lace leaves to the body with a small amount of Royal Icing, overlapping each leaf to give a feathered effect. Mix up the sizes and colours as you go, and finish at the base of the neck. Add a few of the small curved pieces along the back, down the sides and on the head. Leave to dry.

4. Tailpiece. (See Illustration 13). Cut out more of the lace leaves in both colours and different sizes. Starting at the tip of the tail, lay the smallest leaf flat on your board and overlap and attach other leaves with Royal Icing, forming a long triangle. Leave to dry. Dust the 'feathers' with Orchard Violet,Midnight and Viridian petal dusts. Finish with Super Blue and Super Jade Lustres. For the very tip of the tail use the centre section of a lace leaf.

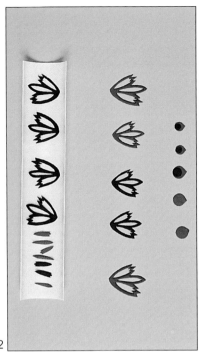

5. Side Decoration - Top Tier. Cut out approx. 20- Green lace leaves LL3 and leave to dry flat. Make the Blue eye pieces with the Mini rose petal R16. (see Illustration 12) Cut out about 20 or so small circles (piping tube) in the contrasting Blue colour and attach to the fat end of the petal. Pipe a small White bulb at the top of the Blue circle. Leave to dry. Attach the top of one of the dried LL3 leaves to the front of the cake with Royal Icing and prop with cloud drift/kitchen roll so that the leaf dries at an angle away from the cake. Attach the remaining leaves at the same height, working to the left of the first leaf until you reach the front again, leaving a gap for the tail. (The mini-turntable is ideal for this job!). Leave to dry. Attach an 'eye' (pointed end towards the top of the cake)above each lace leaf with Royal Icing.

6. Side Decoration - Bottom Tier. Cut out approx. 30- Blue lace leaves LL2 and dry over a curved former or 1" dia.rolling pin. Cut out approx. 30- Green lace leaves LL3 and dry flat. Cut out 30 - Blue rose petals R4 (or R16 to match the top tier). Cut out 30- small Green circles and attach to the fat end of the Blue petals. Pipe a small bulb of White Royal Icing to the top of the Green circles. Leave to dry. Pipe a small amount of Royal Icing to the top of the first curved Blue LL2 Lace leaf and attach to the side of the cake in the front, supporting with cloud drift/kitchen roll so that it dries at an angle away from the cake side.

Attach the remaining Blue lace leaves at the same height, working alternately to the left and right of the first leaf until you reach the back. If it doesn't meet up exactly here it doesn't matter. Leave to dry.

Attach the dried flat Green LL3 leaves in the same way, immediately above the curved ones, and support so that they dry at an angle away from the cake side. Attach the 'eyes' above the lace leaves.

— 9 —

7. Butterfly. Stick the pointed ends of 2 - curved Blue lace leaves LL2 together with Royal Icing and leave to dry. (see Illustration 13) Attach 2 - flat Green lace leaves LL3 to the centre with Royal Icing and support until dry. Make a body with a thin cone of Blue or Green flowerpaste about 3cm(1¼") long. Mark 3 or 4 lines across the body and stick 2 stamens into the head (fat) end. Attach to the centre of the wings with Royal Icing. Leave to dry. Dust with Orchard Green or Blue lustre colours .

8. Covering the 17" board. Cut Blue lining material into strips approx. 12cm wide. Apply Pritt Stick glue to the outer 5cm of the board. Place the strips onto the glued surface and pleat them as you go round the board, adding other strips as necessary. Glue the edge of the board and the underside of the board to about 2cm deep. Carefully smooth pleated material round cake board edge and underneath to secure. Trim any excess material.

8a. Alternatively, cover the board with Blue sugarpaste and roll round the top edge with the 'Varipin' to give a fabric like effect. Trim with a ribbon.

9. Assembly. Place some Royal Icing in the middle of the 17" board and place the bottom tier on top centrally. Place onto the bottom tier of a two tier cake stand. Place the top tier onto the cake stand and attach the tail, either by hooking the top part of the tail through the lace leaves at the end of the body, or (if the cake is not be moved) with Royal Icing, and support with cloud drift/kitchen roll until secure - (a few minutes).

10. Other suggestions. The peacock could be placed in the middle of the cake with the tail fanning out behind.

How to make the Lace Leaf Flower Cake A
(see Illustration 14)

1. Leaves. Roll out Green flowerpaste and cut out the smallest Lace Leaf LL4 leaving a thick portion at the base. Thread in a 26 gauge wire. Dust with Orchard Gold Green and twist to a natural shape. Leave to dry.

2. Flowers. Tape a bunch of stamens, colour of choice, onto the end of a 26 gauge wire. (see Illustration 15)

   Roll out Yellow flowerpaste and cut out 7 - LL3 shapes for each flower. Set 4 over a rolling pin to curve. Before they dry, glue the bases together Maltese Cross fashion. Prop with cloud drift over a large hole in the flowerstand. Glue the bases of the remaining 3 and set them on the wire curved around the stamens. Glue the middle of the Maltese Cross and thread the wire through the middle, interleaving the petals. Leave to dry. (see Illustration 16)

3. Buds. Hook the end of a 26 gauge wire. Squeeze at the base. When dry, dust Orchard Orange at the tips and Orchard Green at the centre.

4. Border. Cut out several LL3 Lace Leaves and leave to dry curled over a rolling pin. When dry, dust the base Orchard Lime Green and the tips Orchard Orange. Put a little paste glue on the base of the cake board and arrange them in threes, two at the back fan shaped and one overlapping at the front.

5. Bow. The bow is the same as for the Bow Cake , but smaller.

14

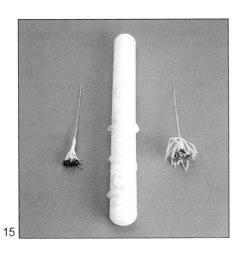

15

16

17

How to make the Lace Leaf Flower Cake B
(see Illustration 17)

by Sue Beck

1. Cover a 14" oval board and 10" teardrop cake with sugarpaste. Place a gold ribbon around the bottom of the cake.

2. Lace Leaf Spray on top of cake.Tape 11 Red tipped stamens onto a 28 gauge wire. Roll out White flowerpaste and cut out 6- LL4 petals. In all cases, when cutting out Lace Leaves, remove all the centres. In this case save the two outer centres from each petal and cover to prevent drying out (12 in all).Glue the inside edge of each of the petals and arrange in an apple tray former to curve. (see Illustration 18)

3. Cut out 5 -LL4 White petals and insert inside the first set of petals, propping with cloud drift to curve. Place the centre cut-outs on the Orchard Pad (PD1). Ball from the top edge to bottom to curve each petal and then place inside the two rings of petals, again propping with cloud drift. Glue the bottom of the stamens and thread the wire through the centre of the flower. Leave to dry. Dust the flower with Orchard Majestic Gold Sparkle. Dust the edges with Orchard Rubine Petal Dust and then steam. Leave to dry.

18

19

4. The Small Red and Gold Flowers are made with the centres saved. (You will need to cut out 7 -LL4 Red leaves to provide the petals for the Red flowers). Tape 5 or 7-fine stamens to a 28 gauge wire. Place a petal flat on the Orchard Pad(PD1) and then roll the Petal Veining Tool(OP2), side to side across the petal to vein and also to curve the petal. Glue the bottom of the petal and place around the stamens. Repeat this twice more so there are 3 petals interleaved around the stamens. Leave to dry. Repeat the above again to provide the 3 outer petals of the flower. (see Illustration 19).

5. The Green middle cutout centres from Step 6 can be used as leaves for the small flowers. Place on Orchard Pad (OP1). Roll the Petal Veining Tool across the length of the Green leaf. Glue the bottom of the leaf and attach to the bottom of the flower. Add 3 or 5 leaves alternating around the wire to finish the flower.

6. Leaves. For the leaves, colour flowerpaste sparingly with Orchard Holly Green concentrate. Roll out the paste on the grooved board and place the LL3 cutter over the vein and cut out. Glue the end of a 28 gauge wire, insert and leave to dry. Repeat this twice more. Cut out one flat LL3 and one flat LL4 and remove centres. Dust with Orchard Gold Green Sparkle. Gently steam all the leaves.

7. To make up the spray, wire together the 3- LL3 Green leaves and place one small flower below the first Green leaf. Place a double loop Gold ribbon on the bottom right hand side. Centre the main flower and then tape together with the wire pointed straight down at the back. Bend the wire backwards at 90 degrees. With a little paste glue on the underside of the flat LL3 and LL4 leaves, place flat onto the cake in the final position of the spray. Attach the wire of the spray to the cake with a little sugarpaste.

8. Side spray. For the flower, tape 11 stamens with red tips and cut out 5- LL3 White petals. Glue the edges of the petals and lay in a curved former. Cut out 5 -LL4 and lay inside first row of petals, propping with cloud drift. For the centre of the flower cut out another 4 - LL4 and cup inside the first two layers, again propping with cloud drift. Glue the bottom of the stamens and insert through the centre of flower and leave to dry. Make 5- Green leaves using LL3 .and dust the whole flower as for Step 3. Similar to Illustration 18. Steam gently.

9. To make up the spray. Wire together the 5 - Green leaves. Add 6 small flowers made up from Steps 4 and 5. Place one two looped ribbon on the righthand side of the spray. Insert the main flower into the middle of the spray. Glue a further 3- flat LL4 leaves flat onto the board. Attach the spray to the board with a small piece of sugarpaste to complete.

10. Place a red ribbon around the base of the cakeboard and lay a gold ribbon through the centre to finish.

How to make the Guy Fawkes Cake.
(see Illustration 20)

1. Head. Roll a ball of Orange marzipan about ¾" dia. Indent for the eyes with the small end of the balling tool OP1. Make a hole for the nose with a cocktail stick. Cut off the end of a piping bag to represent a No. 2 tip and pipe the eyeballs with White Royal Icing. Pipe the pupils, off centre, with brown icing. The nose is a cone of Red marzipan. The mouth is a sausage of Red marzipan tapered at each end and curved to make him smile(or cry!).

   The hair is about 10 thin tapered sausages of Yellow marzipan bent double and pressed onto the head. (see Illustration 21).

   If you have well worked the marzipan at the beginning and are using an Orchard non-stick board, without any sugar, then the marzipan items will stick to each other without the need for additional glue.

2. Hat. Colour of choice. Flatten a small ball of marzipan in a plastic bag, thinning the edge with your fingers and leaving a thicker portion in the centre (otherwise you cannot get it out). The top of the hat is a round ball, flattened slightly. The hatband is a very thin sausage of Brown marzipan, tapered at the ends to make a tiny bow. A liitle straw on top of the hat is made as for the hair.

3. Body. A cone of Brown marzipan, indent for the buttons.

4. Arms. A sausage tapered at the ends. Cut in half. Make a hole in the cut ends (sleeves) for the hands, with a cocktail stick.

5. Hands. A cone of Orange marzipan, flattened. Cut out a V for the thumb and two more cuts for the fingers. Before fitting to the sleeves, push in a few pieces of straw as for the hair.

20

21

6. Trousers. A fat sausage of Brown marzipan. Cut lengthways about ¾ of the way up, bend to the desired shape (sitting or standing) so that the body cone can sit on top. Add coloured patches to the knees. Make a hole in the end of the legs for the shoes. Fit in a few pieces of straw.

7. Shoes. Sausage of Green marzipan, bend at right angles and squeeze at the bend to make the heel. Push into the ends of the trousers. Leave the whole Guy to dry - at least overnight.

8. The bonfire. Cut about 3 Cadbury's flakes into different length logs and stick together with melted chocolate. (The flake chocolate will not melt very well). The flames are the inside pieces of the Lace Leaves, coloured Orchard Red, Orange, Yellow.

9. Flame border. Each group is made up of 1 - Red LL1, 2 - Orange LL2 and 1 - Yellow LL3 curled over a rolling pin and allowed to dry. Glue the LL1 up against the cake with paste glue (see recipe Page 40), the two LL2's on each side, fan wise, and place the LL3 in front.

10. The small border round the base of the cake is made from the inside pieces of the Lace Leaves, coloured Red, Orange, Yellow etc.

11. Add the small decorations, crackers, rocket etc. if required.

How to make the Lace Leaf Cot
(see Illustration 22)

1. Cut out 8 - LL4 White lace leaves and remove the centres. Place 4 of them in an apple tray former in Maltese Cross fashion and glue the tips of the bases together. Paste glue recommended. Repeat for the other 4 leaves and leave to dry thoroughly.

2. Cut out 2 - LL4 and 1 - LL3 White lace leaves and while still soft, glue the 2- LL4 side by side with the larger LL3 placed behind in the centre. Turn one of the dry LL4's from Step 1 upside down, and then glue and prop the assembly from Step 2 on top with the second dry LL4's on top again in the centre. Prop with cloud drift till dry.(see Illustration 23).

3. Mould a tiny baby(about 1" long) by hand or use a mould. Pipe the hair with Royal Icing. Paint the face details with a 000 brush and Orchard dust colours mixed with water or alchohol. Place in the dried cot and cover with a frilled rose petal. Dust to choice - in this case Orchard Rubine and Orchid Mauve.

22

23

24

25

How to make the All-in-One Orchid
(see Illustration 24)

by Sandra Townsend

These quick commercial orchids can be made with any of the Orchard 5 petal flower or calyx cutters.

1. Make a ball of White flowerpaste and press into the largest hole in the Orchard Mexican Hat Adaptor M1. Remove and thin out the brim with the slimpin. Pop the Orchard Five petal cutter F7 over the 'hat' and cut out one flower.

2. Press apart the two bottom petals (see Illustration 25). Bend over the 'crown' between the gap thus formed. Press in the Dresden Tool C halfway down the crown at an angle (curved side uppermost) and press down (see Illustration 25). Smooth the top over the 'hood' of the dresden tool with your finger to stretch the paste. Remove the tool and pinch the 'hood' in a little. Elongate and flatten the labellum by pinching between your finger and thumb sideways. (See Illustration 25). Ball out the labellum on the edge of the Orchard Pad (PD1). Pop onto the edge of a board which has a little cornflour on it and prop the back of the Orchid with the Orchard pad. Frill the edge with a cocktail stick. Place onto a soft sponge and cup the centre with the balling tool.

3. Elongate the top and bottom petals to a point with the balling tool OP1. Ball the side petals from side to side to stretch and smooth. Glue a hooked 26 or 24 gauge White wire and thread it through just below the centre. The hook faces the base. Prop the petals with cloud drift and leave to dry.

4. When dry, glue a little Yellow pollen (Sugartex) to the centre. (This also helps to hide the wire). Dust the edges of the centre with Orchard Carmine petal dust. Holding the top of the wire between finger and thumb, bend the flower to shape.

5. Different Orchids can be made in the same way with any of the Orchard Calyx cutters R11 series to R13A. (See Illustration 26).

6. Leaves. (See Illustration 27) Roll out White flowerpaste and cut out one calyx with Orchard cutter R11F. Cut out each section to create 5 - leaf shapes. Press onto the rose leaf veiner R8. Soften the edges with the balling tool OP1. Glue a 26 gauge White wire and wipe off the excess. Hold the leaf lengthways on your finger and thumb and lay the wire about ¼ of the way up the centre vein. Press the sides of the leaf together over the wire, Open the leaf and bend to shape. Leave to dry. When dry, dust one side Orchard Lime Green and the other side a little of the colour used on the flower.

26

27

28

How to make the Orchid Spray
(see Illustration 28)

1. First tape up the individual branches of the spray with White florists tape.

   Bend the head of each flower forward with a sharp bend to ease taping.

   A -   Tape 2 - F9 orchids, one above the other (see Diagram 28A) and 4 - F7's above.

   B -   Tape 1 - F9 and 3 - F7 similarly.

   C -   Tape 2 sets of 4 - R13 and 1 - R12 Calyx orchids

   D -   Tape 3 sets of 3 - R13 Calyx orchids

   E -   Make 5 individual large F6 orchids.

   F -   Make 5 - Leaves as in Step 6, page 19.

   G -   A small bunch of Gypsophila

   H -   Make 3 - small bows of White ribbon

   I -   Make 2 larger bows.

2. Assembly. (See Diagram 28B). Use tweezers to avoid breakages.

   Bend the bottom ends of the wires of all the branches at right angles to form the stem and tape A and B together, halfway down the stem.

   Tape the 2 - C branches, one each side.

   Add the 3 -D branches at the top. Spread out the branches in a star formation.

   Fit the 3 - small bows behind.

   Place 1 - F6 orchid(E) high in the centre, and the other 4 round it, slightly lower.

   Fill in the gaps with small pieces of Gypsophila

   Tape 3 leaves (F) behind at the top and 1 - each side in the gaps.

   Splay out and trim the wires to various lengths to give a neat tapered stem, then tape down to the bottom.

   Add the 2 - larger bows(I) at the back.

   Cover the stem with ribbon by laying a long piece along the stem, passing it round the end of the stem and then 'bandaging' all the way up the stem This will leave two free ends at the top, which can be tied in a double knot to secure.

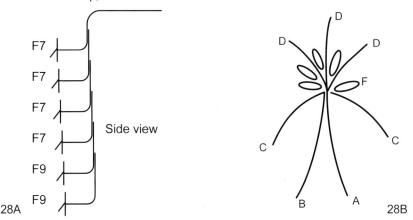

How to make the Lisianthus russellianus.
(see Illustration 29)

Native to America's mid-west, right down to Texas and New Mexico. Flared tulip-like flowers in colours of rich purple, pink, blue and cream. It has lance shaped green leaves.

1. Centre. Glue a **small** ball of Green flowerpaste on to the end of a 24 gauge wire, and roll out into a sausage shape which projects over the end of the wire. Cut down the centre and bend out the two halves to form a 'T' shaped pistil about ½" long. Press each half out in the form of a circle.

2. Stamens. Glue a tiny ball of Yellow flowerpaste onto the end of a 33 gauge wire. Roll to a cone shape and when dry, bend over the wire at right angles. Repeat for 4 more wires and tape them round the pistil from Step 1 onto the 24 gauge wire. Cut out the wires at an angle.(see Illustration 30).

3. Flower. Roll out a sausage of Cream flowerpaste and form a large Mexican Hat with a crown about ¾" dia. Thin out the brim with a Slimpin and cut out 1 - F5 Five-petal flower by placing the hat onto the cutter and rolling with the pin. Put a little fat onto the Petal Veining Tool OP2 (so the paste takes longer to dry and you have more time) and press into the centre of the flower and widen the throat. Elongate the cuts between each petal with a pair of scissors. Vein each petal with the veining tool and soften the edges with the balling tool OP1.(see Illustration 31).

   Moisten the base of the stamens and thread the wire through the centre of the flower. Press the base of the flower gently onto the stamens and roll between finger and thumb to taper the base.

   Dry in a container made from a 3" dia.circle of foil, cut halfway across and curled round into a chinese hat shape. Squeeze around the flower and place into the flowerstand.

4. When dry, dust the base with Lime Green petal dust. The centre of the flower has 5 Lime Green streaks in the centre of each petal about a quarter of the way up.

5. Calyx. Cut long thin triangles of Pale Green florists tape for the sepals (about the same length as the flower). Turn the flower upside down and lay one of the sepals along the flower projecting about ½" along the wire, then tape up the wire. Repeat for the remaining 4 sepals spaced evenly round the base of the flower.

6. Buds. Form a cone of Lime Green flowerpaste onto the end of 26 gauge wire. Cut long thin triangles of Pale Green florists tape for the calyx (about twice the length of the bud). Lay one of the sepals along the bud projecting above the top of the bud, then tape up the wire. Repeat for the remaining 4 sepals spaced evenly round the bud. (see Illustration 31).

7. Leaves. Roll out Green flowerpaste and cut out a A/C1/D1 shape with the 'Varicut' cutter. (See Book 10).Vein with the pointed end of the petal veining tool.

29

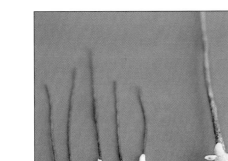

30

31

32

How to make the Viburnum Bodnantense - 'Dawn (see Illustration 32)

This shrub flowers in the depth of winter with tiny pink flower heads, which turn white at the end of the flowering period. They fill the air with a lovely scent. It makes a delightful filler flower.

1. Tube. Pop a tiny ball of White flowerpaste onto the glued end of a 33 gauge wire. Roll between finger and thumb to form a sausage shape. Pull the sausage up until it just overhangs the end of the wire. Indent the end of the sausage with the small end of the balling tool OP1 to make a cup for the flower to sit in. (See Illustration 33).

2. Flower. Roll out White flowerpaste and cut out several blossoms with the F2M cutter. Transfer to the Orchard pad PD1. Ball the inside of each petal with a tiny ball tool (or glass headed pin) to curl over. Turn the flower over, place on a soft sponge and press in the centre to cup. Moisten the centre of the tube (from Step 1) with rose water and transfer the flower (on the ball tool) and press into the centre of the end of the tube. Make an indentation with the pointed end of the veining tool OP2. Pop in the head of a tiny Yellow stamen or paint a spot of Yellow in the centre. When dry,dust the base of the flower with Orchard Lime Green and the petals with Alpine Rose.

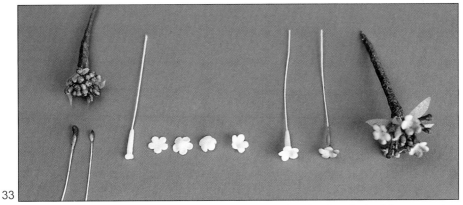

33

3. Buds. Pop a tiny ball of White flowerpaste onto the glued end of a 33 gauge wire. Squeeze the base and roll between your finger and thumb. Dust the base with Lime Green and the top with Alpine Rose.

4. Leaves. Cut half width Pale Green florists tape to leaf shape (See Illustration 33) and tape 3 or 4 leaves to the outside of a bunch of about two dozen flowers and buds with Brown florists tape.

How to make the Chinese Quince.
(see Illustration 34)

1. Flower. Tape about 13 or 14 Yellow stamens to the end of a 26 gauge wire with Brown florists tape.

2. Roll out White flowerpaste and cut out one Five-petal flower F9. Place on the Orchard pad PD1 and vein with the petal veining tool OP2. Soften the edges with the balling tool OP1. Place over a tapered hole in the flowerstand S1 and press gently in the centre with the balling tool to cup.(see Illustration 35)

3. Moisten the base of the stamens with a little glue (rose water) thread the wire through the centre of the flower(supporting the flower underneath with two fingers) until the stamens rest in the flower. Leave to dry.

4. When dry, dust the centre Orchard Lime Green.

5. Calyx. Roll out Lime Green flowerpaste and cut out one calyx R15. Cut off the tips with your palette knife. Widen each sepal by rolling with the petal veining tool OP2. Pop onto a soft sponge and press in the centre with the small end of the balling tool OP1 to cup.

   Glue the centre of the calyx and thread onto the wire, pressing onto the underside of the flower.

6. Buds. Pop a tiny ball of White flowerpaste onto the glued end of a 33 gauge wire. Press around the base. Some of the buds are round and some are slightly pointed. On the larger buds make 5 vertical indentations with the back of a knife. When dry, dust the whole of the tiny buds Orchard Lime Green. Only dust the base of the larger buds.

7. Stalk. Tape together 4 - 24 gauge wires with half width Brown florists tape.

8. Assembly. Tape buds and flowers in pairs down the stalk as in the Illustration 34.

34

35

36

How to make the Fairy Fishing Flower -Dierama pendulum
(see lllustration 36)

Native of Eastern Africa from Kenya to the Eastern Cape. Other names are Zuurburg Harebell, Wand Flower, Fairy Bells or Grasklokkie. In the Royal Horticultural Society's Encyclopedia it is known as Angel's Fishing Rod.

Dainty drooping bells carried on long slender, grass-like stems, arching at the tips with the weight of the Pinkish-Mauve flowers.

1. Centre. Pistil. Tape a small flap of White florists ¼ width tape onto a 28 gauge wire. Cut the flap into 3. Cut each section to a point and bend to form a propeller shape. Paint or dust Orchard Orchid Mauve.

37

2. Put a little Dark Mauve colouring onto a soft sponge and pull through a long length of Scientific wire to colour it. Leave to dry. Cut 3 lengths approx. ¾" long and curve underneath just below the head of the pistil. Tape onto the 28 gauge wire. Cut away the surplus wires. Paint the tips of the wires and tape Mauve.(see Illustration 37).

3. Flower. Press a ball of White flowerpaste into the largest hole on the Orchard Mexican Hat Adaptor (M1) and remove. Roll out the brim and cut out 1 - Six petal flower N4. Put a little Trex onto the veined end of the Petal Veining Tool OP2 and widen out the throat. Holding the base of the flower between your finger and thumb, press against the tool to widen each petal and vein as you go.Pop onto the Orchard Pad PD1 and mark a single vein down the centre of each petal. Pinch the tips. Glue the base of the pistil and thread the wire through the centre of the flower. Pinch the base to secure. Leave to dry in the flowerstand S1.

4. When dry, dust with Orchard Dusky Rose and Orchard Orchid Mauve. Paint small Mauve circles in the middle of each petal about ⅓ of the way from the centre (see Illustration 37).

5. Sheaf. Tape ¾ width White tape from about ¼" below the base of the flower up to the base and then cut a long oval shape to form a sheaf. Dust with Chocolate petal dust.

6. Buds. Roll a small ball of White paste. Hook the end of a 33 gauge wire. Burn the end of the wire with a lighter and press into the ball of paste. Shape into a cone. Make 3 indentations down the length of the cone and dust, mostly Mauve with a touch of Dusty Pink. Make a sheaf in the same way as for the flower, but with ½ width tape.

7. Leaves. Pop a ball of Orchard Lime Green coloured paste into the **centre** of a 26 gauge wire. Roll firmly in the palm of your hands to make a large sausage. Press out the sides with your fingers. Place onto your non-stick board and roll out from the centre to thin out the paste. Move to your Orchard Pad PD1 and vein, first with a dried corn on the cob husk and then mark a central vein with the veining tool.Cut to shape. Soften the edges with the Balling Tool OP1. Gently curve the wire and leave to dry. Dust with Leaf Green. For a stronger leaf, tape 3 - 18 gauge wires to the stem. Steam the flower and leaves.

8. Tape the buds and flowers to a 24 gauge wire.

9. The Fairy. (see Illustration 38) Make a cone from 10g of Skintone lacepaste for the body and elongate it to taper for the legs. Indent three times, cut lengthways and bend legs to required position. Make a hole in the top of the body with a cocktail stick and leave to dry.

10. Make the dress and hat using the six-petal cutter N4. The wings are made with the lace leaf cutter LL4. (see Illustration 39). The arms are thin sausages of paste with flattened hands.

11. Make a ball of paste for the head and use a cocktail stick to make features. Paint in the eyes and mouth with a 000 brush.

12. Assemble the fairy, positioning the head and then the wings. Pipe hair with Royal Icing and dust with Orchard Orchid Mauve and Dusky Rose petal dust.

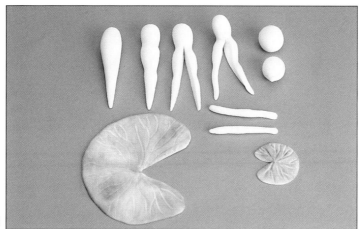

38

39

How to make the Camellia
(see Illustration 41)

1. Centre. Pistil. Roll a tiny ball of Pale Green paste. Burn the end of a 33 gauge wire with a lighter and press into the ball of paste. Flatten the top and, with the tweezers, pinch out 3 sections, in a propeller shape.

2. Tape 4 - 18 gauge wires together with Brown florists tape.

   Tightly wind a piece of rose wire (36 gauge) round the base of a bunch of Yellow headed stamens. Cut off the bottom ends. Pop the pistil into the centre. Tape the stamens (and the pistil) to the end of the 18 gauge wires.(see Illustration 40).

3. Flower. Roll out White gumpaste and cut out 3 - F6C (4") Five-petal shapes. Vein and soften the edges of all the petals with the Petal Veining Tool (OP2). Flap over petals either side. Dust the centre of each petal lightly with Dusky Rose colour, and then put some glue in the centre of the first petal and place the second on top, interleaving the petals. Repeat for the remaining petal. (See Illustration 42).

4. Cut out 2 - F6B (3½") and 1 - F6 (2½") and repeat Step 3, with the F6 petal being on top. Place over a hole in the flower stand to set. Glue the base of the stamens and thread the wire through the centre. Prop individual petals with cloud drift to give a more natural shape to the flower.(see Illustration 43). When dry, dust a little Dusky Rose on the back of the petals.

5. Calyx. Roll out Green gumpaste and cut out 1 - F5 five-petal flower. Widen the petals by rolling with the Slimpin. Soften the edges with the balling tool (OP1). Apply glue to the base of the camellia and thread the calyx up the wire and press gently into position. When dry, steam the flower.

6. Bud. Tape 4 - 18 gauge wires together with Brown florists tape. Roll a ball of White paste. Burn the end of the wires with a lighter and press into the ball of paste. Mark 7 grooves in the paste, to represent the edges of the budding petals, with a knife. Dust lightly with Dusky Rose colour. Cut out a Green F5 five-petal flower, apply glue to the base of the bud and thread the F5 calyx up the wire and wrap round the bud.(see Illustration 42).

7. Leaf. Roll out Green flowerpaste and cut out a 'Varicut' shape A/C4/D1 or A/C3/D1 (See Book10). Serrate the edges with the Petal Veining Tool OP2 by dragging out points around the leaf.

   N.B. The recommended 'glue' for these flowers is paste glue.(See Recipe Page 40).

40

41

42

How to make the Christmas Egg
(see Illustration 44)

1. To make the egg. Use any 5" egg mould - plastic or metal - and polish the inside thoroughly with cotton wool or kitchen roll to ensure a shiny finish. Do not use any other polishing agents.

2. Melt about 2lbs (1kg) of Tesco's White cake covering chocolate in the top of a double saucepan over hand hot water and stir until melted. Heat to a temperature of 38-43° C, or until completely smooth, if not using a thermometer. Fill the mould to the top with melted chocolate. Place in a small bowl to keep the mould upright and leave in a cool place until the chocolate sets round the edge. For a thicker rim, leave to set longer.

3. Pour off the excess chocolate and scrape away any surplus on the face of the mould. Leave to set completely.

4. Repeat Steps 1 to 3 for the other half of the egg.

5. To cut the hole in the egg, dip a 3" oval metal cutter into boiling water and wipe dry. Place on top of the half chocolate egg and allow the cutter to melt its way into the surface of the egg. (See Illustration 45). When it feels tacky, remove from the egg, wipe surplus chocolate off, reheat, DRY and continue the process until the hole is cut.

6. To join the two halves of the egg together, place one briefly on a heated baking tray and quickly press onto the other half.

7. Prepare a solid chocolate bell shaped base, about 2" high, using any convenient mould, and stick the whole egg upright onto the base with melted chocolate.

8. Pipe "Greetings" or whatever on the bell with Red Royal Icing.

9. Roll out White flowerpaste, texture it by rolling it with the Orchard 'Varipin' and cut out 4 - Lace Leaves LL3 and 1 - Lantern L1. Leave to dry.

10. Roll out Green flowerpaste and cut out about 12 holly leaves H3. Vein with the rose leaf veiner R10, twist and leave to dry.

11. Dust the lantern with Copper/Bronze and stick 2 or 3 holly leaves and Red berries onto the top and bottom with melted chocolate.

12. Stick the 4 lace leaves on the outside of the egg symetrically round the opening with melted chocolate. Attach a couple of holly leaves and berries to each lace leaf. Finish with thin Red ribbon to choice.

43

44

45

How to make the Allemanda Cathartica Flower
(see Illustration 46)

Golden trumpet vine. Native to South America. Yellow trumpet shaped flowers.

1. Centre of Flower. Make a ski stick shape on the end of a 24 gauge wire i.e. a small circle bent at right angles to the line of the wire. Glue a small ball of Pale Green flowerpaste to the top, or burn the end of the wire in the flame of a lighter and push into the ball of paste. Press in the centre to flatten. Pinch 4 grooves round the ball with tweezers. Leave to dry. (see Illustration 47).

2. Make a Mexican hat from Yellow flowerpaste using the largest hole in the Orchard Mexican Hat Adaptor M1. Thin out the brim with the Slimpin. Cut out 1 - F6 five-petal flower and open the throat by pressing in the centre with the Petal Veining Tool OP2. Vein each petal with the veining tool and soften the edges with the balling tool OP1 on the Orchard Pad PD1.

   Glue the base of the centre from Step 1 and thread the wire through the centre of the flower. Press the base of the flower gently onto the centre wire and roll between finger and thumb to taper the tube to a length approx. equal to the length of the flower trumpet. Add more paste if necessary, i.e. thread a ball of paste up the wire and mould into the end of the tube. Dry in a container made from a 3" dia.circle of foil, cut halfway across and curled round into a chinese hat shape and placed into the flowerstand S1.(see Illustration 48). When dry, dust the centre Orange and paint random vertical lines of Rubine colour at the bottom of the trumpet. Dust Green on the outside of the trumpet just at the base. Tape on 3 more 18 gauge wires to stiffen the stem.

3. Calyx.Make a Mexican hat, using the second smallest hole in the Orchard Adaptor, with Lime Green flowerpaste and cut out 1 - R13 calyx. Cut off the tips. Place on the Orchard Pad PD1 and ball from the tips to the centre to curl. Turn over and mark in a centre vein down each petal with the pointed end of the petal veining tool OP2. Glue the base of the tube and thread the calyx up to sit just at the base of the tube. Roll between finger and thumb. If using the flower in a spray, fold the calyx onto the tube to avoid breakages.

4. Small Buds. Pop a tiny ball of Lime Green flowerpaste onto the glued end of a 24 gauge wire. Roll between finger and thumb to form a long cone shape. Leave to dry.(see Illustration 49).

   Roll out Green flowerpaste and cut out 1 - R15 calyx. Cut off the tips. Place on the Orchard Pad PD1 and ball from the tips to the centre to curl. Turn over and mark in a centre vein down each petal with the pointed end of the petal veining tool OP2. Glue the base of the bud and thread the calyx up to tuck snugly around the bud. Let some of the buds protrude from the calyx.

5. Larger buds. Pop a large ball of Yellow flowerpaste onto the glued end of a 24 gauge wire. Roll between finger and thumb to form an 1" long cone shape. Roll stem for about the same length. Add more paste if required. Mark vertical curves with a knife which give a twist the bud. Leave to dry.

6. When dry, dust the base Lime Green, leaving the bottom half of the bud Yellow. The rest of the bud is Brown/Dark Orange.

7. Calyx. As for Step 3 but wrap round the bud.

8. Leaves. The leaves are lance shaped,Dark Green. Mark veins with the petal veining tool.

46

47

48

49

How to make the Lily of the Valley-(Convallaria) Majalis
(see Illustration 50)

Although the botanically correct lily has 6 petals, this is a quick and easy way to make it with your blossom cutter.

1. Hook the end of a 33 gauge Pale Green wire. Roll a small ball of White flowerpaste. (see Illustration 51)

2. Roll out White flowerpaste and cut out several blossoms (F2M). Place blossoms on the Orchard Pad PD1 and ball each petal with the balling tool OP1. Pop the small ball of paste from Step1 into the centre of a flower (do not glue).

3. Glue the end of the hook from Step 1 and thread through the centre of the ball. Press in the centre with the Orchard Slimpin. Leave to dry. When dry, curve the wire and tape onto a 26 gauge wire.

4. Buds. Hook the end of several 33 gauge Pale Green wires. Roll various sizes of small balls of White flowerpaste. Glue the end of the wire and thread through the bud. Reshape to a ball. Dust with Lime Green.

5. Leaves. Pop a ball of Orchard Lime Green coloured paste into the **centre** of a 18 gauge wire. Roll firmly in the palm of your hands to make a large sausage. Press out the sides with your fingers. Place onto your non-stick board and roll out from the centre to thin out the paste. Cut to shape. Move to your Orchard Pad PD1 and vein, first with a dried corn-on-the-cob husk and then mark a central vein with the veining tool. Soften the edges with the balling tool OP1. Dry on foil. Leave to dry.

50

51

— 37 —

52

53

54

A Christmas Idea by Stephen Wolff

RECIPES

Flowerpaste A (or Lace Paste)

250g(½lb) Bakel's Pettinice or Craigmillar's Pastello **only.**
1 teaspoon(5ml) Gum Tragacanth

Rub 'Trex' on your hands and knead ingredients together until elastic. Wrap tightly in plastic cling film and store in an airtight container. Leave for 24 hours. Store in a cool place. This paste keeps well if worked through, say, once a week. Always keep tightly wrapped.

Flowerpaste D.

450g (1lb) sieved icing sugar
5mls Gum Tragacanth and 20mls CMC (Carboxymethylcellulose) - Tylose
10mls white fat (Trex or Spry, not lard)
10mls powdered Gelatine soaked in 25mls of cold water.
10mls Liquid Glucose
45mls egg white   **5mls = 1 teaspoon**

Sieve all the icing sugar into a **greased*** (Trex) mixing bowl.Add the gums to the sugar. Warm the mixture in the microwave oven 3 x 50 secs on a medium setting, stirring in between.

Sprinkle the gelatine over the water in a cup and allow to 'sponge'.

Put the cup in hot, not boiling water, until clear.

Add the white fat and glucose. Heat the dough hook beater, add the dissolved ingredients and the egg white to the warmed sugar, and beat on the lowest speed until all the ingredients are combined. At this stage the mixture will be a dingy beige colour. Turn the machine to maximum speed and mix until the mixture becomes white and stringy. Grease your hands and remove the paste from the machine. Pull and stretch the paste several times. Knead together and cut into 4 sections. Knead each section again, wrap in clingfilm, and put into a plastic bag, then in an airtight container and keep in the refrigerator. Let it mature for 24 hours. This paste dries quickly so, when ready to use, cut off only a small piece and re-seal the remainder. Work it well with your fingers. It should 'click' between your fingers when ready to use. If it should be a little too hard and crumbly, add a little egg white and fat. The fat slows down the drying process and the egg white makes it more pliable.

Keep coloured paste in a separate container. This paste keeps for several months.

* This eases the strain on the machine considerably.

Pastillage C.

Make up 8ozs. Royal Icing. Add two teaspoons 'Tylose'. Mix thoroughly. Wrap in cling film and put into an airtight container. Leave 24 hours before working.

Paste Glue.

1oz sugarpaste of the same colour as the items to be glued.
2 dessertspoons of warm water.

Gradually combine together and place in the microwave oven for 1 - 1½ mins until the mixture boils. When cool, use as required. Store at room temperature, or refrigerate if not to be used for a length of time. If the glue is to be used immediately, then it is not necessary to boil it.